TRIUMPH

TRIUMPH
HOW TO SUCCEED IN LIFE

*Wise Advice from
a Great-Great Grandfather*

Ruben Souroujon D'Alcala

VANTAGEPress

This book is dedicated to
Stephanie Souroujon, Alessandra Souroujon, Nicholas Souroujon,
Ellis Bloom, Gabriella Bloom, Liana Bloom,
Ariela Souroujon, James Henderson, Caroline Souroujon,
Dalia Souroujon, Benjamin Henderson, Daniel Souroujon,
Joseph Souroujon and any future
great-grandchildren of Ruben Souroujon D'Alcala

If you want to enter a pentagon,

Don't try by any of its sides;

Look for the sixth.

TRIUMPH

FOREWORD

randfathers and great-great grandfathers are like sacred pillars of history or time, like ancient books, full of information and waiting for someone to come and consult them and learn from them. Whoever consults them acquires knowledge and comes away a stronger person. They can be approached by children, young people and even adults. So, those of us who can turn to them and be understood by them will undoubtedly become new persons.

When we seek out the grandfather or great-great grandfather and find him, it's like meeting an old friend we haven't seen for years; when we see him, we recognize the kind expression on his face, radiating the same strength and the same love, the same accessibility, and, of course, his eternal understanding.

This book is written by a great-great grandfather who has accumulated the experience of his youth, and as he hasn't died yet, wants you to take advantage of this experience. It is not his intention to create a philosophy or to uncover mysteries, or to even transmit wisdom, since this is acquired by the way you live; although it cannot be denied that books help a lot. He is writing this book just to share his experiences, his joys and woes, to share them with grandchildren he may not know or get to know, but he wants to communicate with them.

He's writing this book thinking that the day will come when dawn will break; the day will still be there, the noise will still torment the living, children's laughter and games will still fill the spaces, but he will no longer be there, his space will be filled with silence, a silence that will fill our whole being, but that will not be the end of everything, because his work will accompany those who knew him or have read him.

This book is no more than a way to remain in the world, trying to make it better, for the sun to shine brighter and for us humans to do whatever is necessary to make it more habitable and pleasant. It's a way of reflecting on how to live with ourselves and with others in a more harmonious and sharing manner, knowing that we do not live in isolation, that we all need each other and learn from other people's experience.

David Apolinar Rincón P.

FAMILY LESSONS

WHAT ARE GRANDFATHERS?

A grandfather is a book that children open lovingly.

A great-grandfather is a dictionary that is consulted from time to time, by parents, children and grandchildren.

A great-great grandfather is an encyclopedia we open every time we need it.

A great-great grandfather has so much wisdom for such a short journey on the train of his life.

Only grandfathers have sufficient wisdom to give advice, because of the rights they have earned by getting old.

What makes the grandfather happy is looking back on the whole thorny road he has traveled so far.

There are grandfathers who rejoice in everything they know, but for others everything they have learned causes them pain.

Old people are not astonished when the mermaids sing around a billfold.

Grandfathers do not want "fame"; they know how easy it is for a reputation to be ruined.

They have learned that when we dream we live, because when you dream you learn, which helps to find a solution to your problem.

GRANDFATHER'S COLLECTED WISDOM

Wisdom is a great river that sprang from doubt.

❖

A wise man is somebody who knows where to look for what
he doesn't know, and also to reflect on what he has learned,
to hold it as true.

❖

A great man will always be known for his great deeds,
not for the gossip about his life.

❖

Beauty and goodness always go hand in hand with optimism.

❖

A free man is an ally of the wind and enamored of the road.

❖

How boring to go by the same name from birth to death -
Why don't you change it halfway?

❖

If a woman defeats a man it's a historical deed;
but when a woman defeats another woman it's just gossip.

❖

Every dream will be beautiful so long as it's not interrupted.

❖

History is made by the human beings who give importance
to the past.

The clown sells laughs; the actor exploits tears.

Mature men acquire wisdom at a high price: tears.

Don't boast about reaching forty; you may feel humiliated
when you reach seventy.

No matter how early you get up, you can't make the sun rise any
sooner! Yes, but see how happy you feel when the sun comes out.

He who was born to be a flowerpot will never get farther
than the hall, but how restful he must feel.

Do as you would be done by, that way you'll cry less.

Modesty is man's greatest virtue, but how boring.

Lost your job, huh? Don't worry, this way you'll save on fares!

You got fired? Act with dignity; go and say to your boss,
"Thank you for the opportunity to attempt something better."

A man in front of the Excelsior Hotel in Rome was shining shoes.
He had a very wonderful location for many years, but he was now
an old shoeshine boy. Sometimes you need guts, or even luck, to
change your career. If the Hotel Excelsior had disappeared, or if he
had lost his job, it might have seemed unlucky, but it would have
been the chance to try something new. He might now be an important
executive, or a succesful businessman because he was very smart.

Don't use your right hand to hit your left one.

A politician, what's the point? Any place is good for loafing around, why look for insults?

While there's good money, good food, and good pretty women, life will be beautiful, and what's more, even if there's no money or food, it still would be wonderful.

Sometimes let it go: that girl that snubbed you might have been a disaster !

Love is like a volcano that burns up in its own lava.

Love kisses your mouth, stabs your heart, and eats your money.

What is more beautiful, a white carnation or money?

Every dominant woman will be dominated in turn by fashion and love.

If the alphabet were a woman, there would be fewer illiterate men.

Beautiful women are sometimes the stones in the path of men.

A beautiful woman doesn't worry about being educated so that she can join in the conversations at social gatherings; she is satisfied with knowing she will be the topic of the conversation.

It's easier to melt iron with the warmth of loving words
than a cold woman.

The worst enemy of lovers is the clock.

It doesn't matter what your religion is; what's really important
is that it should instill charity in you.

A man with great faith doesn't need or have time for wisdom.
Fundamentalists of every religion do not rationalize.
Their faith is enough, and they may even kill, or kill themselves.
They only have an obligation to God; the rest has no importance.

If a poor person loses his faith, what will he be able to support
himself with tomorrow?

He who only weaves in his dreams will weave a web of smoke.

Sometimes good lessons are bunches of beautiful lies.

Could it be that judges wear black because justice is dead?

What is a poet? Somebody who dresses lies in beautiful clothing.

Anybody who wants to write poetry must have suffered
at least a little.

There are no bad books, but there are a lot of bad authors.

Very often the self-taught person laughs at pompous university
education; but what discipline he must have,
which not everyone is blessed with.

Just as the master soon forgets the dog's caresses,
so does the human being forget man's favors.

Do you want to know yourself? Enter into the deepest part
of yourself, only in that way will you value your soul.

What man longs for most is to be understood.

Sometimes the spirit is filled with so much good fortune
that it forgets where its soul is.

Every time you look back at your past you will want to recover the
time you lost. If you want to be listened to, keep silent for a while.

What is silence? It's noise without a tongue.

An uncalled-for explanation is a sure sign of guilt;
but at least there was an attempt to distract.
He who excuses himself accuses himself.

The song says… "Wild flower…nobody believes you're a fine
flower since you live next to the prickly pear…" What would the
orchid think if it grew next to the thistle?

If we are at peace with ourselves, why waste our energy
on other people's battles?

If your work overwhelms you, it's because you're
not devoting yourself to it with passion.

Work makes us strong and fills us with pleasure.

When we are most useful is when we make ourselves necessary.

Wealth comes from all the things we give away to our fellow men.

In Mexican culture you can find the gold that Cortes didn't take.

Since you have the chance to wake up once again,
enjoy your new day to the full; it's another opportunity.

Since life is so beautiful, it's pointless to waste it on trivial things.

It's better to suffer than to commit an injustice to get pleasure.

You shouldn't care who did a good job,
it's better to admire the work itself.

What's the point of breathing in a world without hope?

It's better not to talk about someone than to give false information.

If it was so beautiful to be born, why do we insist
on trying to destroy the world?

You only learn the value of time when you take advantage
of every moment of your life.

Fight hard to live and make every moment of your life pleasant
and joyful. But it ain't easy!

If a man has talent he shouldn't waste it on doing harm;
instead he should create ideas that will help improve the world,
only that way will he be a winner.

What is patriotism? Is it love for our country?
No, it's contempt for whoever oppresses it.

Talking about freedom, why are there still so many slaves?

Life is like a race: even if the track is hard,
you must fight to reach the finishing line.

Dear son, grow strong like a rock where the waves break,
that way your family will have peace.

FEELINGS

Sometimes you have such decent feelings that their loss makes you suffer more than the pleasure of having them.

Raul was never self-sacrificing. In his private life and in business he had always been able to defend himself, and was even aggressive. But when Raul fell in love with his wife, he began to suffer.

He sent her poems, he sent her flowers, he took her everywhere and to the best restaurants, yet she remained cold to him. In fact she was frigid, for she was very materialistic. She just wanted to get married; she didn't need love. What's more, she didn't realize how totally selfish she was.

Raul suffered. He tried to spoil her, took her on trips, bought her the most expensive dresses, jewelry, theater tickets, amusements. She accepted everything, but affection and consideration were out of the question.

Raul got to the point where he wanted to get divorced, but even so he made every effort in the hope that one day she would change and show some sensitivity.

One night in Vienna, they had just returned from the opera, where, as always, they had the most exclusive, expensive seats. They went for dinner, danced and drank champagne. When they arrived at the Vienna Palace hotel, where they had reserved the best suite, Raul dared to ask her if she had enjoyed herself.

"Look, why do you ask me? You know it's quite normal for a gentleman to spend money when he loves his wife. But I would have liked to be in Budapest, where there are more things to do and better nightclubs.Now I'm going to bed and please don't bother me. I want to sleep in peace. And tomorrow please don't forget the earrings that you promised to buy me. Good night."

Raul thought hard about it, taking his time. He counted to ten and then to ten again... and he slapped his two hands near her face as hard and with as loud a bang as he could.

"Starting tonight I am the boss. Please say thank you and move over, I am going to bed with my wife!"

That was the day when Susana finally fell in love and learned to respect her husband. ⊛

FAMILY ADVICE – CHOOSE WISELY!

Do you have a wife, kids and more serious problems every day? Has your wife become ugly, your kids unbearable? Is your life becoming very complicated?

Dear friend, if things are going badly for you it's your fault; you treated your pretty young wife badly, and didn't give any attention or time to your children while they were young and still impressionable.

"Just a minute, great-great grandfather," you might respond. "That's not true. I did everything perfectly and it turned out badly."

You're right. It's possible, or should I say probable, that you didn't take her genes into account when you got married. You married for money or for a beautiful pair of legs, or an angelical face? You picked the prettiest girl, the town's beauty queen, and you didn't pay attention to her genes?

What were her parents like, what did her brothers and sisters look like, what were her grandparents like? Were they good-natured? Were they normal, affectionate, cheerful?

Their genes are the ones you chose for your wife and for your children. There's no changing them. Don't have any illusions; you chose the genes you're going to live with for the rest of your life. ✪

MORE FAMILY ADVICE – BEWARE!

Sometimes you find the worst specimens in the best families.

When it is a question of the inheritance, family love goes to pieces.

Beware of the people who say they are your best relatives; they may be the worst snakes.

The worst thing in a good family is that the brothers and sisters sometimes hurt each other.

You say your mother-in-law is the worst. Come and spend a day with mine so that I can ask you what you're complaining about.

The best mother-in-law is the one that lives 10,000 miles away.

Why do poor people have so many children? Because this is the only fun they can afford.

COUPLES BECOME FAMILIES

What about couples, what about marriage?

First of all, there must be communication, even if it's shouting, but they must never stop talking. Silence as a form of torture is the greatest stupidity. It shows that the person who uses it is a real idiot.

There are a lot of imbeciles. And a lot of divorces. Meanwhile, take care of the family.

The sons-in-law, the sons, the daughters-in-law, the daughters. Hand over the money and keep your mouth shut. The grandparents, the parents-in-law, the brothers-in-law and other in-laws...Put up with them.

The family is a very nice institution but sometimes it's disturbing. Put up with it. ✹

THAT'S LIFE,
ACCORDING TO GRANDFATHER

The future will be better than the past,
and everybody should give it a try.

The decision not to do anything is also a decision.

He who is too afraid to start something is doomed to failure.

I love animals, particularly dogs. Sometimes they seem human,
or is it me who's becoming like an animal?

Every conversation is an adventure, and very often a discovery.

The 30th of February should be
proclaimed International Faithfulness Day.

Is it true that old people cry because
they no longer have anything to laugh about?

The most delicious thing in life is having lived with what we love.

It's a fifty-year-old love story. And I still love her.

GRANDFATHER'S
NEW
IDEAS

LIFE IS SHORT,
YOU'LL SOON BE 60

Now you're twenty, twenty-five, or forty years old. Poor you! Soon you'll be sixty.

You'd better start programming yourself for that date right now.

Enjoy life now: you'll discover that after sixty, your body has ideas of its own and your mind is no longer the boss.

Meanwhile, you're going to face social, family, health, sex, and money problems.

You'd better learn from the experience of a few old folks who have been sixty many years ago.

Here are some examples of what they've learned:

When you fall in love you become stupid.

If you get married, try to avoid somebody with more problems than you have.

It ought to be very difficult to get married
and it should be very easy and simple to get a divorce.

Men married to nice women are happier
than those married to women who are just beautiful.

You fall more in love after you are married than before,
but nobody believes that.

The pretty girls already have a boyfriend...
and the ugly ones become pretty when they find one.

SUNDRY IDEAS

The more you give, the more you will receive.
Sounds illogical, but that's the way it is.

Love is like a soccer game where both sides commit faults,
shoot goals, can win or draw, united for the next encounter.

When you have nothing to lose you can risk everything.

Have you thought that sometimes you think too much?

There's something you can never buy: Time! and Love.!

Don't complicate your life. What's the point in bathing your goldfish?

There's talk of abolishing capital punishment. Great!
Let the criminals start first.

The jails are full of innocent people;
could that be why there are so many criminals outside?

Look, never insult a crocodile until you have crossed the river.

You know what? Discipline is eating just one potato chip.

Being optimistic is like the spring.

I also love you because of what I become when I'm with you.

Time wastes our bodies and our wits.
But we waste time, so we are quits.

Yesterday has already happened, and who knows what will happen tomorrow? But TODAY is "cash" – take advantage of it!

Do you know that today is tomorrow's yesterday?
Somebody told me, I don't remember who.

I'm an idealist; I don't know where I'm going
but I'm in a hurry to get there.

When you're on holiday, you have all the day to do nothing.
When you are retired you have no more holidays.

If you want to approach somebody without much difficulty,
just smile, this is the shortest way.

I'm not better than you, but neither are you.

Whether you're a king on a throne or a Mr. Nobody sitting on a chair, it's all the same, you're sitting on your behind.

You get sick earning money, then you spend it all on getting better.

It's really silly to be superstitious. It brings bad luck.
But what's the cost of touching wood?

PHILOSOPHY OF KINDNESS

I want to stay alive, until I die.

Do you want to have a lot of fun, real fun, with a good conscience and at no cost whatsover?

Then buy yourself a cap. And when you are in your car and you see a pedestrian, raise your hand to let him cross, and then with the same hand on your cap, give him a little wave. If you drive a Mercedes Benz or a Cadillac, or any other car in that category, I promise you the reaction will be one of surprise, particularly if it's a humble person. Can you imagine what he will have to tell his wife and children when he gets home?

And, what did it cost you? Nothing but more fun.

But how much money do you have? In cash, investments, property; one million, five million, ten million? I swear I have nothing to do with the Treasury Department or Income Tax IRS; what's more, if you don't want to, don't tell me.

You will agree that you have a thousand, or possibly a hundred thousand, times more money than the poor devil you see pushing a wheelbarrow in the street or the single mother begging for money. Those poor souls don't have any more than ten, maximum fifty, pesos in their pockets.

Now tell me, honestly, how would you feel if you won a million pesos in the lottery without ever buying a ticket? Just like our beggar would, if he receives fifty pesos or one hundred pesos from a complete stranger (a peso is a twentieth the value of a US dollar).

Don't hesitate! Indulge in these small kindnesses. I promise you you'll go to heaven! ❀

THOUGHTS

There's something funny about life: if you always seek the best,
sometimes you find it.

Don't be content with less than you deserve;
then they give you even less than you accepted.

Women won their rights and lost their seats on the bus.

You treat your employees as your equals...
and then they believe they are.

My father used to say that the only thing he liked about rich
people was their money.

You're very decent, you treat a girl with the greatest respect,
and nothing happens. Then along comes a good-for-nothing
and sleeps with her.

Men distrust women, and women distrust women too.

It's difficult, almost impossible, to be halfway honest.

Don't keep on talking about how honest you are.
That's irritating. Thieves don't tell you about what they've stolen,
and they risked a lot more than you ever did being honest.

❀

I get on very well with people;
the person I've had a lot of problems with is me.

❀

I admire Mrs. Bollinger. Her grandfather launched the Bollinger
brand of champagne. She said, "I drink champagne when I'm
happy and also when I'm sad. Sometimes I drink champagne when
I'm on my own, but with friends I consider it a must. I play with
it when I'm not hungry and drink it when I'm hungry. Apart from
that,
I hardly ever touch it...unless I'm thirsty." The only thing
I regret now is not having drunk more champagne and enjoyed
this life more to the full.

❀

My only successful creation has been my children,
and in fact that was just procreation.

❀

Having sex on your brain is no use at all;
besides, it's not in the right place.

❀

Tell me who you love and who you desire,
and I'll tell you how things will go well or badly for you.

❀

If you want a bargain, but a real bargain, marry for love.

❀

They always say you should treat others
as you would like them to treat you.
Yes, but what happens if his tastes are different from yours?

❀

Do you want to know a person's character ? Invite him to a buffet.

❖

The word is a dangerous weapon.

❖

With human beings, I prefer to talk to a kid or a Finn
or a Chinese person because there are no words
and the conversation is just smiles.

❖

We love animals a lot because they don't talk.

❖

If my little dog Freddy is happy, he laughs with his tail.
If he's sad, his eyes tell the whole story.

❖

A dog will never make fun of you, criticize you,
or try to convince you that he's smarter than you,
that you've put on weight or that you look older.

❖

Have you noticed? We're very similar to a goat tied to a post
with a rope to prevent it from straying from its field.
But we have a hammer to drive in our own stake.

❖

Dear doctor, the last thing I want to do is to die.

GOD

Everything started in California with an eggplant that had a very distant resemblance to Richard Nixon's face.

There was quite a stir. What a coincidence. What a fantastic likeness! Fate, luck, belief in something inexplicable. You tell me, how many eggplants are there in the world? A lot, I can assure you. How many stones are there on our earth? Billions, trillions, and when somebody finds a rock that looks like an Egyptian Sphinx, we make such great fuss about it.

You know what? You can take a million monkeys, the smartest ones if you like, and get them to hit the keys of a million typewriters for a year. If they happen to form a coherent phrase or word it will be a miracle.

And Shakespeare, what?

In this life nothing happens by chance. Everything is well-organized. There must be a Supreme Being that organizes everything.

It's not possible any other way.

God does exist! ❋

REFLECTIONS

In the end we are all equal,
but some are a bit more equal than others.

Generous people are generous with their money and with their
feelings. And likewise, cheapskates are stingy with their feelings.

How old would you be if you didn't know your age?
You'll never stop growing even if you're very old.

You change jobs, friends and wives,
when really the only person you should change is yourself.

Be confident, you know more than you think.

If you take great care of yourself and don't want to take risks,
you're like a ship that never leaves the port.

You have dreams, fantasies, but for these to come true,
first you have to wake up!

The most important things in life?
You know what, they are not things at all.

The Internet is as good as a lot of journeys.
But it's less tiring and much cheaper.

Everybody says I'm lazy.
It's not true; it's just that I rest before I get tired.

Look, you shouldn't take life so seriously;
in any case you won't come out of it alive.

Sometimes it's a good idea to speak in a low voice.
Nobody can hear you and everybody thinks you're right.

When you get really angry, it's as if you're driving a racing car:
you accelerate without knowing that the brakes don't work.

Just because a girl is pretty doesn't mean she's not intelligent.

If one day you like a girl, tell her so, she won't get bored with
people repeating it. Socrates (or was it Plato?) said it.

People who applaud me don't bore me,
even if they repeat themselves…

A person who marries for money would have found it cheaper
to ask for a loan.

Those who say that money isn't important
are usually those who have a lot.

Being honest is so exceptional that you can do fantastic business,
because you don't have any competition.

You can be taught everything,

it's just a question of time, money and patience;

but enthusiasm, that you either have it or have not;

you can't buy it.

If you rob a thief, you don't feel so bad about it;

but it's easier to rob an honest person.

When you accidentally fall into the river,

you're no longer a fisherman but a swimmer.

Sometimes I give myself good advice; but I don't follow it.

At the end, life ain't easy.

HOW
TO
SUCCEED

HOW TO SUCCEED IN LIFE!

It isn't easy to be successful. There's so much competition. So many people are smarter, better looking, richer and more attractive than you.

So why is it that suddenly you see an ugly, fat, bald man or, if you are a girl, a woman who isn't as pretty as you are, who is the center of attention and feels very sure of themselves?

Is it true? Have you noticed it?

You know what? They have all the right methods for success!

They know how to speak, dress, and smile. There are so many basics and so many tricks.

Would you like to begin to work with me?

But first some considerations.

It is stupid to expect other people to do what we can't do ourselves, but people who do well are those who earn the right to have the beautiful, good things in life. Their courage sometimes springs from the depths of fear.

Maybe you find you have many personalities within yourself, but you only have one soul, and you can't change that.

When you set out to do many things and don't decide on any of them, you end up doing nothing.

Don't worry about living many years; it's better to think about living life to the full.

Money doesn't buy happiness, but it helps as long as it does not go to your head.

So, now let's work on how to succeed socially. ❂

FAME

I like to travel first-class, but it's hard to earn money. Working is a solution, but it's very tiring. However, traveling the world in the lap of luxury is enjoyable, and it seems like celebrities get everything given to them.

So:

How can you become famous?

Write a book? But everybody does that and the competition is terrible.

Kill twenty-four people or assasinate somebody very famous, but then they don't allow you to travel.

Win the Nobel Prize; it's not a bad idea because you earn both money and fame.But you have to work really hard, and they give you the Nobel Prize twenty years after your work or discovery.

In the end, the easiest way is to start a business.

Michel has no capital, barely enough to pay for a week's vacation in Palm Beach, the richest city in the world after Monte Carlo. But he's surrounded by so many millionaires, something should come out of it.

He hired the latest model of convertible and went to the bank. "Please change this hundred-dollar bill for fifty new two-dollar bills." He put them in his billfold, being careful not to fold them so that they would stay completely new. Now he felt like a "two-dollar bill millionaire."

Michel went to visit the City Plaza, the Breakers, the Ritz Carlton and the Boca Raton Resort and he noticed something: each of the millionaires in their Jaguar, Mercedes Benz, BMW or even Rolls Royce, gave a one-dollar tip when the valet brought him his car.

Everywhere he went Michel gave a new two dollar bill.

It so happens that nobody has realized that you can go to the bank and buy as many two dollar bills as you like, and that they are always new because nobody has thought of asking for them. Also, people who are a bit superstitious do not spend these bills; they keep them hidden in their billfolds because they bring good luck and a good chance of making a fortune. You can imagine the kind of service Michel received! His car was always brought to him before the others and with a big smile.

One day, at the end of his vacation, a middle-aged man waiting for his Rolls went up to him and, seeing that he was so popular and also young, invited him to his yacht.

"Look young man, I'm Mr. K. and I'm the owner of the this resort, which cost me a fortune. Now I want to buy an elite hotel in Palm Beach. I've noticed that you get on very well with people and that you have a slight French accent. I'm going to give you credentials from a real estate group in Paris. They're friends of mine, and with that high recommendation you're going to visit Mr. S., the owner of the hotel.

"It is the most important and luxurious hotel in the world. The Ritz is nothing in comparison. I want to buy it, but if Mr. S. finds out I'm interested, he's going to kill me and ask an exorbitant price. Your job, together with some Novotel employees who will arrive from France, is to find out at what price he would let it go. He knows the French are tight-fisted but he wants to sell.

"It is a question of negotiating. I'm talking about hundreds of millions of dollars. Don't get scared, here in Palm Beach County it's normal to talk about large figures.

"Get me the hotel at a good price and I promise you will be rewarded. The negotiations may take weeks, but don't worry, I'll pay all the expenses."

The negotiations took a month of hard work, but Mr. K. was very pleased with the results. He invited Michel for a coffee and liqueur on his yacht and said: "Congratulations! I knew from the moment I met you outside the hotel that you had an exceptional personality and you have an extraordinary sense for public relations.

"Everybody likes you. We're going to do a lot of business together. Here's a check for you. I hope you think it's enough. But tell me Michel, what's your secret?"

Michel took the check for two million dollars, folded it and put it in his pocket. Then he took out his billfold where he had his last new two dollar bill and showed it to Mr. K. "This is my secret."

Now, dear reader, I beg you to believe what I'm going to tell you. Even though it sounds incredible and as if I'm making it up. It's the truth, I swear! Do you know what Mr. K. said to Michel?

"Please, can I keep it?" ✸

BUSINESS

It pays to be rich.

It makes everything easier, even your self-confidence.

It's almost impossible to get rich if you work in a company where you're not the owner. While you're waiting to start your own business you have to learn by working for somebody else and prepare to become independent. Of course, you have to start somewhere. Try to find a job where you have the possibility of becoming the owner of a similar business very soon.

Logically, if you work for a bank or the Government it's going to be difficult for you to set up your own business, unless you go into politics or you are a financial genius. But look for a small or medium business in an area that interests you. You have a greater chance of learning how to set up your own business before you are thirty.

Let's take an example. You like the clothing or footwear industry and you think your future could lie there. Then let's say you look for work in a shoe factory and start to work like the devil in manufacturing, sales, and administration, so that you become indispensable. Now's the time to go out and start up your factory, even though you may start out in a very small way and will have to work ten times harder than before.

Just remember one thing. Twenty or fifty years ago somebody started this empire from scratch. Why can't you? ❀

HONESTY

Try to be honest. That's not so easy, because every day there are fewer honest people.

But don't think that people are stupid; there are others who are at least as smart as you. It's not a question of you being smarter, or maybe you are, but what is most likely is that you have more imagination.

The other thing that you will have, and the others, at least not all of them, won't have, is honesty.

Only honesty will lead you to success because it is so rare. ⚙

LOOK PEOPLE IN THE EYES

They say that the eyes are the mirror of the soul.

It sounds easy and very simple. However, sometimes you're embarrassed or you forget.

One way to remember this habit is to look for the color of the eyes of the person you're talking to.

It's such a simple trick and yet so many people look the other way, out of shyness or lack of interest, or because they think that the person in front of them is too important. Often you'll notice that these important people look away. It doesn't matter; keep on looking for the color of their eyes.

It's a strategy; sometimes you'll notice that there is fear in the eyes of the people to whom you feel inferior, or that you admire so much. They have their problems, just like you, and the eyes reflect their anxieties.

In the eyes you also may recognize the queen of deceit: hypocrisy. The mouth may tell lies, but the eyes will always betray the truth.

If you discover a fault, a lack of security, I beg you not to take advantage of it. On the contrary, be the model of compassion. I won't forgive you for being proud and disdainful.

Arrogant people are a pain in the neck. Don't be arrogant, and if you are now beginning to succeed in society, don't let it go to your head, don't get all presumptuous and rude. You have the advantage, you've read this book.

But who knows, be careful, they may have read it too. ❀

IN SOCIETY

You've finally gained self-confidence after so much hard work. Now try and look as if you have achieved everything naturally and effortlessly.

I'm going to tell you a secret; don't tell anybody. Do you meet people and celebrities who scare you? Are you prepared but still not sure of yourself? Yes?

Rhythm! Rhythm! Rhythm! That's the key. If you can make sure you always have rhythm, then you've won the game.

Start in easy situations, with friends or your family. You're in an easy environment, try it out! Think: Rhythm! Rhythm! Rhythm!

Ridiculous, isn't it? Why didn't you think of this before? It's so easy, and all of a sudden you've got rhythm, even when you are asleep.

Rhythm! Rhythm! Rhythm! Repeat to yourself until you get it into your head that it's easy to act with rhythm, even when you are scared and panicky.

I can promise you that at first you'll fail. Keep on until it becomes the most natural thing in the world.

What should you talk about? Don't pretend to be something you're not. Talk about a film you enjoyed, a magazine article you found interesting. Please don't try to show off.

But don't let yourself be taken in by other people showing off their knowledge. Don't follow up on a topic that seems artificial and affected.

"I've read Kent, Schopenhauer and Bergson, they're fantastic."

Yes, yes...

"I saw a movie with Marilyn Monroe, very amusing...It was fantastic!" ❀

FRIENDS

Do you want to have friends? Real friends? They should be at your social level. Not higher or lower.

Beware of celebrities, millionaires, princes and other creatures who believe they are superior to you.

I can swear that no millionaire ever gave me a million dollars because I tried to be his friend. Trust my experience. Nor will a prince give you a title of nobility, or a celebrity a passport to glory.

Please, don't build up your hopes; those people are superior, or rather they feel superior. For them you're a lackey and they have no consideration, unless they need you. However, it may be in your best interest to use them, knowing perfectly well that you are the one who is using them.

I'll give you an example:

I knew a prince and I sent him to open doors in all of the countries in the world, with heads of state, with political leaders, the owners of very large companies. They all were snobs and tried to make a good impression on high aristocracy, thinking possibly it would rub off on them. Real social climbers.

I paid him very well. Together we made a wonderful team. But the prince did not see why he needed me, so he went alone. Why give away fifty percent? As it turned out, he got one-hundred percent of zero, as I had the experience and the know-how. We were doing very well until he set up his own business, and went bust. ✸

EATING, DRINKING AND MAKING LOVE

D on't rack your brains. The technique is a guide, but with practice it will make you perfect.

There are thousands of books on manners and etiquette for dressing well, eating well and showing that you're a man of the world.

Buy a book, any one, and read it, study it, and practice what it teaches.

The rest is just rhythm, even making love…even Eskimos sweat when they make love. ⊛

HOW TO DRESS

Do you want to succeed or not? Then make an effort to look good. It looks easy to dress well. But it isn't if you intend to be successful, because what you have to do, man or woman, is to find your style.

Your physical appearance is part of your overall image. But it can be improved by the way you dress.

It can be sporty, elegant, or even hippie if you like, but it must be clean and attractive.

If you have a beard it should be clean; if you have long hair it should be neat. You may make an effort for it to look disheveled, but it has to be on purpose, because it's your style, not because you're lazy.

Even if he's ugly, a well-dressed man will always look good. Don't be afraid to look good. It pays! ❀

FEMININE APPEARANCE

If you're a woman, sparkle, or splash yourself with very cold water after showering and before putting on your makeup. Ice would even be better. You will get the twinkle.

Use a perfume you like and which is distinctive to you, but it must be DISCREET.

You have class, and that naturalness it took you so much effort to achieve.

I think you've understood me. If you haven't, then it's been a waste of time. Sorry, my friend. ✸

AT PARTIES WITH GIRLS –
ADVICE FOR BOYS

Messages on napkins are good: if you don't make out with the girl,
you make out with the waitress.

❖

Ask the girl you like to dance. If she says yes, then she likes you;
if she says no and you offer to accompany her to her table
and she accepts, then you have a chance.
If she says she's with some friends, you have two options:
if she's with girlfriends, try again;
if she's with men friends, leave.

❖

If you see a girl who is moving to the beat of the music
and has already turned away several men,
then either she's sad or she's waiting for you to make a move.

❖

If you are with a group of friends and several girls start
dancing together in front of your table, go up to the one you like
and ask her to dance. Please believe me, they prefer a man,
any man, rather than a female partner.

❖

Try to be a good dancer, they like that.
Always, being able to dance well is the key to success.

❖

And if you dance, dance, don't talk.

❖

WITH BOYS –
ADVICE FOR GIRLS

If the boy you like doesn't take any notice of you,
walk in front of him.

Dance with a girlfriend in front of his table.

If you really like him, don't be shy.
Men are not so sure of themselves; they don't really know what
they want and like to be pushed.

If he doesn't ask you to dance, ask him yourself.
In fact you can smile, you've got nothing to lose.
Your dignity? Forget about being a dignified spinster.

Don't drink.

If he offers a drink, let him buy you the next drink.
If he doesn't, just pay for your own and give up hope.

If you dance better than him, don't let him notice.
If he dances well…show off!

FOR BOYS:
DATES WITH GIRLS

When you go out with a girl, let her talk…
if she doesn't, invent a topic!

On your first date don't tell her everything about yourself,
you lose your mystery. After the dessert talk to her about a short,
interesting subject she doesn't know about.
Sports, movies, theatre, fashion. Anything except YOU.

Try to have a sense of humor, and avoid sounding pompous.

Be friendly and respectful.

Always show up for a blind date, even if you never see her again.

When a girl meets a boy, she already knows what she wants
him to be: a friend, a boyfriend or an unlimited source
of outings and money. Try to learn which category you fall into
as soon as possible.

Show discreetly that you know about good food and wine,
everything from a quesadilla to a gourmet meal…
Knowing a lot about wine is very dangerous and very expensive.

If you have money problems, make it clear;
they don't mind paying occasionally.

Never take the girl to meet your family on the first date,
she'll think it's formal and will keep her distance
even if she likes you. Same for the opposite sex.

If a girl cancels a date with you, but postpones it for another day,
you're lucky.

After three refusals, forget it...she isn't interested.

MORE ABOUT DATES: FOR GIRLS

If he asked you out it's because he likes you. Don't start to make an effort and try to dazzle him. We're not stupid.

Dress suitably for the occasion and the place.

If you want to learn about his standard of living, look at his shoes.

If you want to snub him, just look at your watch from time to time.

Look him in the eyes.

Try to sit close to him.

At the table, touch his arm occasionally, they like that.

Let him talk, they're very vain.

Try to find out what topics he's interested in beforehand; then you can innocently ask him to talk about them.

Pay attention to what he's telling you.

Never guffaw, just laugh or smile.

Tell him you have to leave, but stay a little longer.

PHYSICAL LOVE

The difference between man and animals is that for them caresses and kisses do not exist. Sorrows, lovesickness, we can drown them in a glass of tequila.

The variety of physical beauty is what adds spice to life, but at the end, it makes you less rational, and you become stupid.

I have learned more from your face than I have from my own. Why did God make you so beautiful? No doubt it was so that you would glitter and madden me with your sparkle. ❁

LOVE

You can love, be in love or pretend to love, be obsessed or think that you are in love and loved in return.

Don't worry, you're young; you have to love, it's essential, but you also have to eat and breathe.

So you ask yourself, what then?

Love is a necessity but it must be mutual. It is not a one-way street.

You are so much in love and somehow you feel that your loved one is your soul mate. Excessive, crazy, exaggerated love, whatever.

Heed this advice. Never! I repeat never! Without exception, love somebody who doesn't respond or doesn't love you. ✸

MARRIAGE

Don't get mixed up with married people, don't get involved, whether you're still single, or worse, if you are married!

There are so many single men and single girls. You don't need to get mixed up with somebody who's married. Never. No excuse.

Even if she tells you her husband hits her every day or if he says he can't stand his wife any longer, don't get involved!

Stay away! ✸

HEALTH

The following recommendations are the opinion of the author alone, are not warranted as medically accurate, and are not intended as a substitute for professional advice from a physician.

Health first.

None of what we've been talking about will work if you don't have good health. You can have all the will in the world; make every effort to follow my advice.

Sick?

Forget it. If you don't enjoy good health, it's a thousand times more difficult to be successful.

"It's easy for you to talk. But I feel tired. I can't sleep; I get one cold after the other. My bones ache. I'm constipated. My head aches. Don't talk to me about health. Don't you think I would like to be as healthy as the rest? Don't tell me you can help me. I'm very sick!"

OK! OK! Don't get angry. Trust me and you're going to get well.

What's your problem?

Have you got a good doctor? If you have enough money, go for a complete checkup and I promise that anything, if you take care, can be cured.

If you don't have money it's more complicated, but even so, there's a way.

Suppose your doctor tells you that you have cirrhosis of the liver, but you're not sure that his diagnosis is correct or if his treatment is right. Get a second opinion. Don't feel bad about it. If your doctor is offended, too bad. Your health is more important than any considerations about his feelings.

OK, now you have two opinions but you're still not very sure; you want to know more about your illness. Go to the Internet and visit Google and enter the name of the illness they diagnosed. One click and you have ten pages with information. The symptoms, the treatment and the medications that are suitable.

If you don't know anything about the Internet, ask a friend to help you. It's a way to check; if the answers don't match, the diagnosis was wrong. Visit another doctor, until you are satisfied.

Or you can show your doctor the research you have carried out and ask him if he wants to change his opinion. You need a lot of courage to do that, but if you like, you can suffer in silence.

Please understand that you're the only person in the world who knows how you feel.

VITAMINS

You take multivitamins? They're not enough. Buy Vitamin A (Beta Carotene), Vitamin B Complex, Vitamin C and Vitamin E.

Vitamins A and E are not soluble, which means you have to limit their intake. For example, 15 000 units of A and 400 mg. of E every day.

But all of the rest are soluble, so you can indulge.

If you have the time, read the books of Dr. Linus Pauling. He was very sharp and died when he was ninety-two years old, half a century ago, when reaching eighty was a phenomenon. The only man in history to win two individual Nobel Prizes, Dr. Pauling recommended 6000 mg. of Vitamin C a day and an excess of Vitamin B Complex, ten times higher than the normal dose. He believed that if there is an excess it will be dissolved in the water we drink every day. We'll have the most expensive urine in the world, but it is possible that these macrodoses will serve to protect against cancer and vascular disease and help cure constipation and digestive disorders.

He may be right. I know vitamin addicts and they seem to do very well. Take this seriously and investigate about vitamins, minerals and supplements.

If the General Nutrition Center Corporation (GNC), which has 10,000 stores all over the world, has earned millions of dollars and sells billions of vitamins a year, it must do something right and have something to offer. I don't think there would be so many millions of customers if they weren't offering something worthwhile.

Believe me, trust me, and look into this, please. Don't say no without investigating first.

DIET OR LOVE?

You read a lot about cholesterol and heart disease recently. Now you have to be careful about what you eat, avoid fats, sugars, proteins or any other type of food you may like.

But you know, in the Mediterranean countries people eat a bit of everything, they have fun, and then die at a ripe old age. Aren't they lucky!

What is it? Could it be the wine, the olive oil, their good humor, or because they make love a lot? It would be worth checking that out. ❀

SPORTS

They're a great way of keeping fit and in shape. But for them to be effective, you need a lot of discipline.

Discipline is the key. Don't be lazy about choosing a sport; it's a great way to make friends and contacts.

However, you have to follow some well-defined codes of behavior.

TENNIS

Above all, look as clean as possible; your tennis shoes must be clean. The color doesn't matter.

At the end of the match shake hands, even if your opponent is the worst cheat and the most obnoxious person ever.

If you play doubles, give your partner just compliments, never advice or a scolding. If it's mixed doubles, a kiss.

GOLF

What's most important is to dress well and have good equipment. Never, but never, move the ball, even if nobody is watching.

Talk about golf, not business; that will come later at the nineteenth hole.

AT THE POOL

Wear a bikini only if you're young and have a perfect figure. There's nothing more sad and pathetic than to see a mass of fat wobbling between the two halves of the bikini. It's better to wear a one-piece swimsuit with a little skirt. The same goes for the monokini: only if you have the right figure.

As for men, it's just too bad if you're bulky. Try to lose weight.

OTHER SPORTS

Skiing: very fashionable. If you don't know how to ski, take classes until you can do so reasonably well, because a novice on the slopes is a danger to himself and to others.

Horse riding and jumping: have a good horse you can control. ❀

FREDDY THE HERO

Freddy is a male sausage dog. He has a lot of personality and we love him a lot. He likes people and other dogs too, although he's still very young.

Who would have thought that this dog would change our lives and save us from a very dangerous situation?

How would he do it? What was the danger? There were no risks of a fire because the building was built to be fireproof. A terrorist attack wasn't very likely since five armored guards protect the buildings where we live. And do you think a bandit or a criminal would be afraid of that sausage dog that still had not even learned how to bark?

It was a Sunday afternoon. We had recently adopted that extraordinarily intelligent dog, with an indisputable pedigree. You could see the gratitude in his sad little eyes and his family dog loyalty, a first-rate dachshund that in fact preferred German shepherds. We joked about it. Could it be the language?

Sally and I were slouching on a couch after attending a concert, and we had rather too much for lunch. Freddy was pretending to sleep on the mattress, but in fact he was planning on saving our lives.

Freddy pooped on our best, newest rug.

Sally and I put him on his leash and went out into the street to walk him around the block. Every two hours we had to go down and walk around the block, an exercise we had never before considered.

After two weeks, our ten extra kilos began to go down to six, and then four, thanks to this new activity. We even plucked up courage and went on a diet, and took up tennis again.

When we saw the cardiologist a month later, he said to us "I am amazed. You were on the point of having a heart attack because you didn't take care and look after yourselves. I congratulate you on your discipline, you saved your lives!"

Freddy! I wish you had been there to hear it. It would have made you very happy. ❀

A PRAYER

Written in 2002

Dear God, today I've reached eighty.

Thank you, thank you very much for giving me such a long life.

But please, let me live one more year to enjoy my grandchildren…

However, there could be more grandchildren and I have so much to do; could you give me up to eighty-two?

Do you think I will still be alive when the new model of the Jaguar comes out?

It seems it's going to be extraordinary!

If I'm still alive, why don't you let me drive it for another year?

Look God, if I make it to eighty-five, I promise you I'll give a fantastic party, even if I'm broke.

Dear God. In 2008 the Olympic Games will be held in Beijing.

It would be really wonderful to see that Chinese show on the television.

It will be the greatest show of the century; it would be a pity if I missed it.

And then I'd be 87.

It would be marvelous.

Thank you, thank you very much.

But could I have one more year?

It will be my golden wedding anniversary with Nelly.

They were fifty years of happiness.

It would be only right to celebrate.

After that, dear God, I promise I'll be ready to go.

I promise!

God was kind and gave me all these years. Now, in another prayer, I ask for five more years! Am I abusive? ✸

ADVENTURES AROUND THE WORLD

THE BEAUTIFUL REDHEAD

When I arrived in Mexico on vacation, long before I met my wife Nelly, I suffered a foreigner's usual problems.

I went to the Sanborns de los Azulejos and asked for a coffee and a "gato." I meant "un gateau," a pastry in Belgian. But in Spanish it is a cat. A very attractive girl in traditional Mexican Chile Poblano dress explained to me that they did not serve cats there. "I want a coffee and a gato," I exclaimed, showing off my perfect Spanish.

The girl called the manager, a very intelligent young man, who understood that I came from a different and distant land. He very politely explained to me that in this country they don't serve cats, and least of all in Sanborns, a very chic restaurant.

"I want a coffee and a gato!" They had to call the assistant director, a middle-aged man who spoke English perfectly. We understood each other right away. "No problem," he said, and they served me the most delicious cake I had ever tasted.

Another example is when my mother arrived from Europe.

The day she arrived, which was the Monday after Easter week in 1954, the peso was devalued from 8.65 to 12.50 on the dollar.

Anyhow, relatives and several friends went to the airport to meet her but with long, sad faces.

My mother was really sorry about the circumstances that coincided with her arrival and her first words were "Estoy Embarassada." She intended to say, "I am embarassed." But in Spanish it is "I am pregnant."

By then she was all of 65. What a faux pas! First they were shocked and then they all laughed until they cried - the first smiles on that awful day.

Also, it was quite common for well-intentioned friends to try to improve my Spanish pronunciation. They made me repeat a hundred times: "Rápido ruedan las ruedas del ferrocarril." The many r's were to be rolled and not gutteral. I repeated it a thousand times but could never manage the trilled "r." Never.

However, the problem I suffered most from was the Mexicans' habit of asking each time we met, "What can you tell me, Ruben?" I never knew what to say and would rack my brains to find something to tell them.

At the get-togethers of young emigrants, there was a red-haired Mexican girl with big, bright eyes. I wasn't in love with her and I don't even remember her name, but every time we met she greeted me with, "What can you tell me Ruben?" And I had to answer something.

At that time I was honest! One day I told her I had fallen off a horse, another day that I'd seen a terrible accident on Paseo de la Reforma. But it was difficult to find something to tell every time. Once I dreamed I'd been run over by a train and I woke up feeling very happy.

Then one night when I couldn't sleep, I suddenly found the solution.

The next time I saw the beautiful redhead approaching, and before she could open her mouth I grabbed her by the shoulder and I almost shouted: "Hola Lolita, what can you tell me, Lolita ?"

Very calmly she looked into my eyes with her big gray-green eyes. Beautiful eyes. Taking her time she thought it over and answered, "What can I tell you?" Then slowly and very deliberately she added, "Whatever you tell me, Ruben!" ✹

TANINUL

Six months had gone by and I set off in my convertible to get a new tourist visa.

In those days the road to the United States crossed the Sierra Madre through the Huasteca. After a dozen bends, going uphill and downhill, I got a flat tire and was stranded alone in the desert. Soon men, women, children and old folk began to come down from the mountains and crowded around me to see what had happened.

"The truth is," I said, "I'm not very good at changing a tire."

Seeing how incompetent I was, a young man offered to help me. In fact, he did everything - not very well, but ten times better than the driver.

As I was still basking in financial glory at that time, I took out my billfold and gave him an enormous tip in dollars. I must admit he appreciated my gesture, particularly when he calculated how many pesos that represented.

Meanwhile, more people came down: all poor, all rather wretched. But they were friendly, smiling, not at all dangerous. I closed the trunk, said goodbye to everybody, and the same young man gave me a big Mexican hug to say goodbye and thank me for the tip.

Just as I was ready to leave, an old man – at least he looked old to me – asked me if I would be passing through Taninul. It was the father of the young man who had helped me, and of course I agreed to give him a ride to Taninul even though it was out of my way. His wife would accompany us.

They really were a decrepit, dirty couple, a bit out of keeping with this new yellow convertible, a latest 1952 Chevrolet, and with such an aristocratic driver. However, all of the natives expressed their thanks for my compassion and, like a hero from The Odyssey, I sat the old lady in the rear seat.

The man, ready to sit next to me, said goodbye to his son. But I noticed something strange: the son winked discreetly at his father and put something I couldn't identify in his right pocket. During the entire seventy-kilometer journey he kept his hand in that dirty, disgusting, tattered pocket.

Surely it wasn't a gun: if that was his intention I wondered why they hadn't killed me at the beginning of the journey, in the desert.

Finally we arrived in Taninul, but the old man didn't want us to go into the hotel because his workmates would have made fun of him, seeing that fancy car and not the bus. So he wanted to go out into the open desert.

His wife stepped out and he said: "Thank you, boss." And he put his hand back in his pocket.

Coup de grace! No, no, it can't be…

He took out his hand and gave me my billfold. "Yes, boss, it fell out of your pocket and my son asked me to give it to you."

Not one cent was missing. ✸

ALWAYS ON SUNDAY

The idea was simple: I loved Mexico. How could I help Mexico without it costing too much? A school, a hospital, a palace – I had five children, and with their extremely expensive school fees, forget it.

I painted a red heart, the symbol of love, and little by little it began to crystallize in English: "I love Mexico," but instead of "love," it was expressed, "I ♥ Mexico." The letters in green and the heart in red.

I had a hundred posters made, then a hundred bumper stickers. I gave them away. That was my contribution and my way of saying thanks to Mexico.

Who knows what they did with the posters. My office was the best customer. But the bumper stickers really did catch on, and you saw cars in the street with that caption.

Somebody said to me, "Bravo! You obviously love Mexico, but put it in Spanish." Easy! I just had to change "I" to "Yo," and I had a thousand made. Now they were noticeable. When I launched ten thousand, the city looked really patriotic; "Yo ♥ Mexico" could be seen everywhere.

One morning I got a call from Raul Velasco's secretary. He wanted to interview me about my beloved stickers, so I went to his office on Reforma Avenue. From the outside it was obvious that this was somebody important because of the number of guards and controls at the door. And when I went in I realized it was some kind of film or television company from the number of beautiful young girls, all Hollywood material!

Raul, an extraordinarily charming young man, explained that they had found my phone number through the Embassy, and he wanted me to present my original drawings and ideas personally on his program "Always on Sunday."

Why shouldn't my wife come too?

The following Sunday we went to San Jeronimo and, after passing through several controls, they put us in a room full of costumes, furniture, and decorations, under the stage from which we could hear singing, shouting, applause, and loud noises. After half an hour I lost my patience. I gave a pack of posters to the girl who was looking after us and we said goodbye.

Imagine our surprise when I got home! We had several calls from friends and acquaintances who had seen us on TV. How was that possible? It seems that just that day, the famous singer Emmanuel had been on the show, and fifty million people had watched the program.

Raul Velasco, who was really smart, interrupted the program to show the "Yo ♥ Mexico" signs, mentioning the name of a Belgian who had fallen in love with Mexico, and his very beautiful wife.

When he knew we had fled, he took a shot of the backs of a young couple and exclaimed, "Look, my friends are so modest, so shy, so patriotic, that they are running away from the TV. I couldn't catch up with them. But I got a shot of them on camera!"

Fifty million people saw my back and the beautiful nape of my wife's neck. ✦

A TRAIN JOURNEY

Michel had some business in Geneva and took the TGV Train at the Gare de L'Est. It's very pleasant; he enjoys spending two or three hours reading in a reclining seat, and then goes to the restaurant to enjoy a meal of fish, usually Dover sole, well-served and with a bottle of Pouilly Fuisse.

Michel has this habit: always, on planes, trains, or even in the bus he sometimes takes in Paris, he tries to sit next to an attractive woman. His theory is a very simple philosophy: in the event of plane crash, a collision or a derailment, it would be much nicer to crash in good company.

He's over sixty years old, has traveled a lot for his job as a petrochemical engineer, and has never had an accident, although sometimes he has wished for one.

The woman in the dining room on this occasion was attractive and elegant. She looked very young, no more than twenty-five, with new, good-quality clothes. Rich people recognize each other; they always wear new clothes, new shoes, everything of the best quality, but without being ostentatious. Without this type of people, the drycleaners may go out of business.

There were four people at the table: a gentleman, a middle-aged lady about Michel's age, and the girl. The conversation revolved around the train's speed, when they would arrive in Geneva, the usual. Nothing personal.

However, the girl seemed interested in Michel. He was impressed, and started to make jokes and amuse his companions with funny anecdotes, but in good taste. What really surprised him was that such a pretty girl should make conversation with him, show an interest, and laugh at all his remarks. She asked him which hotel he would be staying at in Geneva: the Hotel du Rhone, which she knew very well.

Very charming, and surely without any wrong intention, she asked him to accompany her to her house, which was in the most aristocratic neighborhood of Geneva.

"Frankly, I'm not good-looking, or that young" – Michel thought to himself – "Well, better like that, maybe she likes me, or maybe she's suffering from unrequited love. Even so, she looks very happy and doesn't seem to have any ulterior motive."

The taxi ride to the outskirts of Geneva was uneventful. Alice, that was her name, told Michel about her studies, her plans and how happy she was to have met him. He behaved very well, hoping that he could take the initiative again once they arrived at her home. At least a little kiss to start off with. He knew Swiss women were very liberal as far as their feelings are concerned, and the upper class ones even more so.

She invited Michel into the house, a little palace. A good sign. Her parents had gone to the theater. She offered him a drink, better still. He was beginning to build up hopes, sitting there together, on that magnificent sofa, the perfect atmosphere for a flirt. Too good to be true.

Just then they heard a forced laugh, a senseless laugh, the laugh of a rich person who wants to make a good impression. And coming down the stairs, behind that tight, artificial laugh, appeared an old lady dressed disco-style, with a miniskirt and a tiny transparent low-necked blouse. She was at least Michel's age, that was for sure. Her face, like a dried prune, full of wrinkles, many times operated on, and her neck stretch-marked like a piece of creased cardboard. And wearing a young girl's skirt and blouse !

"Michel, I'd like you to meet my grandmother," said Alice, taking him by the arm and dragging him towards that grotesque apparition. "You know, from the moment I met you I liked you. You obviously have a lot of class and you're very charming. I'm sure my grandmother will like you. She's very lonely. Why don't you invite her to a good restaurant and then go dancing? "

"Excuse me," said Michel, "but I'm very tired, and I'm going to bed. Good night and have fun." ✸

MOZART

In Vail they have built an open-air amphitheater called "The Gerald Ford Theater" after President Gerald Ford, who pardoned Richard Nixon after Watergate.

There are covered seats, protected by an artistic roof, but no walls, and behind, large areas of lawn where music enthusiasts can gather and have a picnic while they listen to the top musicians of the season.

From any angle you can see the mountains, the parachutes or handgliders, and at the end of each concert the sun sets at the appointed time. It's ethereal.

Yes, there is still a corner of paradise in our corrupt world, and the celebrities seeking anonymity feel protected from publicity, even though they're among such a large number of people.

It's an unwritten rule that you shouldn't try to get familiar if you are sitting next to a Senator or Bill Gates. But here they chat with you, knowing that you are ordinary people, just like them. And if you are Carlos Slim they don't ask you how many companies you bought last week or, if you're Carlos Fuentes, how your last novel was received. You talk about tennis, golf, how brilliantly young Kim played the piano or how sad it is to see Isaac Perelman looking so worn out. So, Princess Diana talked about her sons and the problems they had learning French, and Elizabeth Taylor about her last pneumonia.

In fact, the only people who were in the public eye were President Ford and his wife Betty, They were very discreet, but at the beginning of the concerts their presence would be mentioned, and then they would stand up and greet the audience in a friendly manner. They were pleasant and tolerant, just as I had imagined them.

The bodyguards sit at the back, very discreetly, but if Jimmy Connors goes to the restroom with his little son, suddenly two giants have to go too.

At one philharmonic concert, the soloist was a famous young French violinist called Emmanuelle Radivert. From the beginning of the Mozart Sinfonia Concertante everyone realised her genius, though she was so young. But because of the wind that was blowing across the hall, her skirt was falling open.

Undoubtedly she had brought this elegant, modern, beige silk dress from France; it combined perfectly with her white lace stockings and her shoes, the same color as her dress with high heels and a strap. She was unconsciously very sexy. It just happened that her dress was a wrap-around and the wind revealed that, perhaps due to the heat, Emmanuelle was not wearing any kind of underwear.

Poor thing! She had never expected that she would be performing in such a windy hall. Even so, she played the allegro with an enthusiasm and technique that only a world-famous virtuoso could master.

The first movement ended, the orchestra was resting, when suddenly a figure appeared on the stage. It was a well-dressed woman, wife of one of the millionaires from Aspen, Colorado. A well-known moral advocate, this lady went up the stage and straight to the young woman and, with a determined swipe, slapped her hard on the face.

Nobody had time to react; after all, it was the wife of an important figure, and the orchestra started the second movement, an andante. With her beautiful face sparkling with tears, Emmanuelle Radivert played the movement with sentiment, talent, and technique that none of the members of the audience had ever experienced before.

The hall became a temple. Some people were crying, others were praying, it was like a spiritual happening. The symphony ended with a lively allegro and the whole audience rose to their feet to applaud. The members of the orchestra were on their feet clapping their palms on their instruments when Emmanuelle calmly put down her violin and bow on the floor and let her dress fall off next to them.

Completely naked except for those white stockings and those sexy shoes, the girl showed her appreciation with a slight bow of the head. There was an overwhelming ovation, uninterrupted cries and exclamations.

Then Emmanuelle Radivert took her leave with a deep bow, bent over, picked up her violin and her dress, and walked slowly towards the dressing rooms. ✺

THE CAP

In Mexico City, which is at an altitude of over twenty-five hundred meters, the sun's rays are very dangerous and can cause cancer of the skin. Fortunately, there's a lot of pollution, which filters the ultraviolet rays. But even so there are occasionally some clear days and it's better to take precautions.

Dr. Owens recommended I should wear a hat, and I found a white leather cap in Mr. Tardan's store. After a few months I got used to it, and even went to the movies wearing my cap. So once when I was in Switzerland, I was wearing my cap when I met Nelly's Aunt Mutzi for the first time. She's a lady who talks a lot but she's very smart and the whole family heeds her advice.

"Pleased to meet you Michel, you look great in that hat, very bourgeois, very strong, very Swiss. Why don't you wear it to one side? That way you will look younger, more intrepid. But don't overdo the angle. If you do you will look like a bandit, or a ruffian. I like to see you looking a bit sassy, a lady-killer, cheeky, but not shameless." When Mutzi speaks you do as she says.

On my way back to Mexico via New York, I had problems at customs. It was the first time ever they opened my suitcases, and they searched me as if I were a drug trafficker. That would also be the last time, because now I take off my cap before the plane lands in the United States.

In Mexico it doesn't matter. I look normal. This cap has a life of its own. Sometimes it's very successful. The girls are either frightened or impressed, depending on its tilt. Yesterday a girl nearly had an accident because she wasn't looking where she was driving – she was looking at me!

However, the cap had its moment of glory in Houston.

Why did I have to rent a Cadillac? Just to show off, so what? When I got to the freeway exit for the airport I had to stop at a red light. Suddenly some kind of giant approached me with an evil expression on his face and a stick in his hand. He didn't even give me time to close the window. He got closer and closer, I could almost smell the stink of drugs on his breath.

A reflex, adrenaline, made me tilt my cap at a reckless angle. It was the only thing I could think of. The raging lunatic stopped, with the stick already raised, and in a broken voice, full of hatred, he shouted, "Damn! These bloody gangsters from New York. I don't mess with them." ✸

POEMS

THE WIFE

Sometimes in a marriage there's so much love
That you have no desire to cheat on your wife.

Sometimes, it's possible and overwhelming
For you to find her so lovely and delicious
That all the stars in the world, movies or TV
Pale in comparison, and only leave you cold.

Yes! I love you, you love me and I adore you. ✤

FATHER'S DAY

Fathers deserve to be celebrated, too.
Mothers are proud that they have
A good husband, and the children,
A good father who supports them.

How nice!

He works for the whole family
And he deserves all our love.
He's the one who guides us,
Maintains and conducts us.
And we respect him so much
Since, after God, he's the boss. ❈

MOTHER'S DAY

If you have millions, but no love in your family,
You are poorer than the man with the wheelbarrow.
He, every day, enjoys his father and his mother.

A mother, more than all the yachts and palaces,
The banquets, the parties, and the empty honors,
Teaches you values, which are important in life.
And you know what, those values never are things.

Now you have millions and you have a mother.
She gave you good luck and she's wonderful!
She'll give you more dazzling moments of joy,
And her only wish is, that you, also, love her. ✪

LOVE

Have you loved and then lost?
Have they broken your spirit?

Have they loved you without hope?
And you in turn have also betrayed?

Is there such a thing as shared, painless love?

You love God, and does God love you?
Ask him to give you a bit of extra love.

Scatter that love to the four winds;
You have a lot, you can be generous.

And suddenly you earn the dividend
Of being loved and loving in return. ❁

GREAT-GREAT GRANDCHILDREN

The children in my family
Were born amidst great joy,
But they grow up so quickly.

Too soon they'll become old
And grandfathers themselves.

But how can you slow down
The years that go so quickly?
How can you make them last,
At least, last until you die?

Please don't say goodbye yet.

Why don't you pray: " Dear God,
Please help me find a lasting love."

This will be the only solution,
Because in life and also death,
There will be no end to your passion ❀

CHILDREN'S DAY

April is the month
Every year.
When children rejoice.

When children sing.
When they are good,
And then misbehave,

You can't see the reason
For their changing moods.

We don't care. We love them anyway,
And always more on children's day.

TANGO

It's the tango of a computer
That suddenly became crazy;
His hardware was so in love,
He became completely stupid.

She was a pretty, classy laptop
That usually rested on his knees.
A sexy beauty, with such skill
That his kneecaps went hip hop.

But she wanted more software.
This is the sad tango of a lover.
That laptop gave him frostbite,
And he finally died of despair,
Because he lost all his megabytes. ❀

THE COMPUTER

It's enjoyable, but you need a lot of patience.
It's an animal, intelligent, yes, but opiniated.
You can be tolerant but not compassionate,
Because it won't show any compassion for you.

It won't forgive the slightest error you make.
And worse still, the computer rebels for no reason,
As if it was my fault. And, as a dictator,
It just decides to erase everything you wrote.

Please don't take it personally,
But don't have any illusion:
This computer is a real sadist
That would love to torture you,
If by error you take it seriously. ✸

LOVE AND MONEY

In this hell of a life
I was alone.
All was pain
And sorrow.

But when I started to make money,
I became sweet, and very popular.

"Don't get old without money,
Honey. "

God! Why is life so complicated? ❁

GOD...AND LIFE.

He who prays is really asking God for an advance.

It's easier to pray than to serve God with kind deeds.

God is very busy, but God is omniscient.

So have no illusion: you cannot fool God!

DON'T EVEN TRY. ❁

SPEECH

Before I speak,
I have something important to say.

It's easy to begin a speech,
But it's very difficult to end it.
It's like conceiving a child,
Which is easy, but later
You have to pay for his education.

So, I think I should end my speech before I begin. In any case I
have nothing to say.

Thank you!
Rubén. ❂

THE END

I'm tired now.
Life is beautiful but very short.
Succeed today! Not tomorrow! ✷